Back In The Game

"My Observation and Assessment
of our Two Major Political Parties
and President Obama"

Beverly Montgomery

BEVERLY MONTGOMERY

ISBN-13: 978-1514752159

ISBN-10: 1514752158

BACK IN THE GAME

One Woman's View of Our Current and Past Presidents
And the state of the
Democratic and Republican Party

DISCLAIMER

The material for this book is based primarily on my perception of the Democratic and Republican Party accomplishments, failures and other observations.

DEDICATION

This book is dedicated to my friends and family. You have always been steadfast in your support of me. I love you all unconditionally.

TABLE OF CONTENTS

INTRODUCTION   1

CHAPTER ONE   6
Barack Obama – My Observations

CHAPTER TWO   11
The Issue of Credibility

CHAPTER THREE   16
Barack Obama – Under Fire by Some
in the African American Community

CHAPTER FOUR   22
My Early Memories of the Office
of President

CHAPTER FIVE   29
The Early Years of our Political Parties

CHAPTER SIX   34

Early Roles of African Americans
in the Republican Party,
Early Parties and Presidents

CHAPTER SEVEN   49

Accomplishments and Failures

CHAPTER EIGHT   72

The John Boehner Factor

CHAPTER NINE   75

The 2008 Elections and Key Candidates

CHAPTER TEN   82

2016 Elections and Candidates

CHAPTER ELEVEN   106

Impact of Racial Issues on Politics

ABOUT THE AUTHOR   109

BEVERLY MONTGOMERY BOOKS   111

BIBLIOGRAPHY   113

INTRODUCTION

I entitled this book "Back in the Game," because I provide my views about why I believe the Republican Party was able to regain political dominance in 2014 and become the majority party in the House and the Senate.

Additionally, I discuss the similarities and differences as well as issues and accomplishments of both the Democratic and Republican Parties.

But most importantly, because there has been a lot of rhetoric concerning President Obama's job performance, I provide my personal views on what I perceive to be his successes and failures when compared to other Presidents throughout history.

However, the title of my book can also be applied to experiences in my own personal life or the lives of others. In the past, I often allowed setbacks to hold me back from doing things because I felt that I either didn't have the power or resources to make them happen or I allowed someone else to make me feel that I was not qualified to do them. However; this is no longer the case and in the last ten years, I've been on a mission to establish a number of rigorous goals that I've not only brought to fruition, but in many cases, I've far exceeded my goals and I've achieved feats that I would've previously thought impossible.

Undoubtedly, there are some people sitting on the sidelines hoping for my failure, but I count them amongst the few and irrelevant. I no longer depend on others approval because I finally know that I possess the abilities and drive to attain the goals I set for myself and I will let nothing or no one get in my way.

Though I do value others opinions, ultimately, someone's opinions of me will never be the determining factor for the choices that I make in my life. That's why I decided to write this book. It's out of my comfort zone because I'm more comfortable writing fiction novels and children's stories. However, I refuse to put limits on myself.

Therefore, I will cover a number of political issues which I feel are relevant and important and directly related to the successes and failures in both the Democratic and Republican Parties. Since we're rapidly approaching the end of President Obama's final term in Office, it's my desire to have open and honest dialogue and hopefully get people excited about voting in the next election.

It's time to stop criticizing President Obama for what he has and hasn't done during his two terms as President of the United States. At this point, it is far more important to get off of our behinds and champion the right Democratic and Republican candidates for the 2016 elections. But when we elect our next President, let's afford them an opportunity to make some mistakes without jumping all over them. Everyone makes mistakes and I'll discuss this more in other chapters of my book.

Let he who has never made a mistake stand up and take a bow or better yet, put it on the internet so the world can see that you're a liar because it's simply not true. If you're human, you have made lots of mistakes so let's find a way to support rather than tear down the people we choose to lead us. Better yet, I read a quote recently that said, "If you've never failed, you've never tried anything new," and that about sums it up for me.

People are far less forgiving of others when they make mistakes for having the courage to try new things or implementing ideas and changes that are controversial. Prior to researching information for this book, I believed that the Republican Party had never represented all people, however;

my research opened my eyes to the facts, myths and fallacies that exist with regards to the Republican Party.

For example, in 2010, the Republican Party had a very strong foothold in the political arena, but several events contributed to their steady decline in power and their dominance in the political arena.

But in order to have a full understanding of the Republican Party and Democratic Party, it was necessary for me to go back to the early years of our Country. I particularly wanted to fully understand the impact and role the Republican Party and Democratic Party has had in the minority community and the country as a whole.

I must say that quite a bit of what I've learned has been very enlightening because I'd previously only allowed myself to be open to the doctrine of one party and that is the "Democratic Party."

It is not my goal to have my findings sway you in one way or another because that's not the intent of this book. What is important for me is to present the facts as I perceive them to be, no matter how cold or raw they may appear. My ultimate goal is to lay out my beliefs on why I feel the Republicans were able to make a series of fumbles that caused them to lose their dominance as a party only to regain it.

They did this by capitalizing on a series of mistakes and poor judgments and decisions made on the part of the present and past Presidents and other key policymakers and representatives in the Democratic Party.

CHAPTER ONE

Barack Obama – My Observations

As Barack Obama's Presidency nears an end, it has become increasingly important for me to make my own assessments of his job performance and accomplishments.

My desire is to address some of the issues and stumbling blocks that have been placed in his way from the beginning and throughout his Presidency.

I must say that what I've observed from the outset of his Presidency is President Obama's ability to carefully orchestrate the way he desired to be perceived by his supporters and non-supporters by trying hard to be a President for all people. However, it has been very hard for him to keep the promises he made along those lines because he couldn't avoid the fact that he was dealing with real life issues from a variety of special interest groups. That's why, I

6

don't believe that President Obama fully understood the challenges that he would be confronted with on so many levels.

It's difficult to please everyone and especially when there are so many special interest groups vying for his attention and approval of their agendas or programs. Though he hasn't necessarily succeeded in this area, it's not because he hasn't worked hard at it.

Sometimes, the best you can do is to do the best job that you can for the benefit of all rather than focusing on a specific group of people. But with all that he has accomplished in his Presidency and his record as a Senator, there continues to be those that believe that he shouldn't have been elected President in the first Place.

In fact, Dick Cheney claims that Barack Obama is the worst President in history. While I don't believe that to be the case, I also know that there are a great number of people who feel that way privately. Too bad, that so many people have allowed their prejudices to hold them hostage for so many years. It is simply a travesty, blatant bigotry and wasted energy. From the very beginning of Barack Obama's first term as President, some right wingers have challenged his citizenship and birthplace and have attempted to make it a large factor throughout his Presidency. Whether or not it has had any negative impacts on his Presidency remains to be seen, but it certainly has consumed far too much of his time in challenging these claims. No other President in history has come under so much scrutiny as has Barack Obama. He has been criticized at every turn for making decisions that he has deemed best for our country.

But in some cases, Barack Obama has gotten in his own way, however; nearly all of our Presidents have had their share of problems and controversies in both their personal lives and in their political careers.

In fact, most if not all of our Presidents, have done or said something stupid including having awkward moments that have caused people to wonder, "What was he thinking?" However, what people fail to understand is that these people are human and no different than you or I in that respect.

The big difference is that elected officials are in the public's eye and represent the United States of America on so many different levels.

As a result, they're held to a higher standard. Because of this, he or she needs to be more transparent and always aware that we and the world are watching them. They represent every American so it's important for them to be seen in only the very best light. However, as you'll discover in this book, none of our President have been beyond reproach. Therefore, it's important that I'm honest in my assessment of President Obama… giving credit for the things that I believe have gone well for him while identifying things that I believe haven't gone so well.

The truth is…my assessment is only one person's view of his job performance and doesn't mean a hill of beans in the real scheme of things. I can't nor do I want to speak for the Country or the world. I'm merely sharing my observation of this President's job performance.

I will also touch on other topics and issues, including the Democratic and Republican Party struggle for political dominance. Most interesting to me is the fact that over the years, leaders in both the Republican Party and the Democratic Party have both made their share of mistakes and it has cost them greatly.

In some cases, the mistakes have adversely affected the very people that the leaders of these parties have purported to represent. But in 2014, it was the Republican Party that was able to make a comeback and regain political dominance as the Majority Party in both the House and Senate.

This too, had to do in part to many Americans disdain and dissatisfaction with Barack Obama. I honestly, believe little of this dissatisfaction is directly related to Barack's actual job performance. I think much of the backlash against President Obama has had more to do with simmering issues due to bad race relations in our country.

These feelings have always been there and though we sing com bayou and proudly sing America the Beautiful or the Star Spangle Banner at big events, the truth is we have a very long way to go particularly, when one race believes that the color of their skin gives them clout over other races.

CHAPTER TWO

The Issue of Credibility

Never in history has there been so much talk about one President's credibility and qualifications for the job. Not even George Bush, the 43rd President, has come under so much scrutiny.

The reason I chose George Bush, 43rd as a comparison has little to do with the fact that he held the Office of President prior to President Obama, but more to do with the fact that though he was the Governor of Texas, from my perspective, his experience as governor, did little to prepare him for the job of President. I distinctly recall the day of his inaugural. I couldn't help but notice that as George Bush emerged from the limousine to a cheering crowd, he walked with his wife Laura Bush and made it a point to stand tall and straight with his shoulder back, seemingly hearing his mother's voice saying, "Stand up straight George." That left an indelible impression on me because it showed vulnerability and a strong desire to make a great impression.

But that brief moment also showed me that he wasn't quite comfortable with his new role and I believe he was probably thinking about the huge responsibilities of the job. However, at that moment in time, he appeared to want to portray the portrait of a strong and confident leader.

Unlike President Obama, George Bush had the luxury of having a great resource in his father, George Herbert Bush, our 41st President. If he desired to, he could bounce things off of him not because he needed someone to help him make decisions but it's always great to get another person's perspective on important issues.

This is particularly true, if that person is someone that you admire and love. His father had to be an incredible resource for him. I would argue that like most Presidents, George Bush 43rd learned a lot on the job. However, people were more forgiving of his mess ups and laughed at him when he did or said things that were not appropriate for the situation. A great characteristic in President Bush 43rd is that he has a great sense of humor and would often laugh at his own mistakes or gaffes. But let's be real, it has been well documented that President Bush 43rd was an average student in college and he had a problem with alcohol in his younger years but was able to completely stop abusing alcohol in 1986.

As Governor of Texas, there was a lot of controversy around his beliefs and exercise of the death penalty in Texas, where he approved the execution of over 153 death row prisoners at the rate of one every nine days. His record of executions far exceeds any other Governor in the State of Texas.

No doubt, some of these prisoners might have been proven innocent of their accused crimes had he not been so eager and willing to push the executions through so rapidly. Though President Bush 43rd gets major credit for his handling and involvement in the 9/11 crisis, there exists a glaring stain on his record as President.

This is attributed to his lack of adequate attention to the Katrina catastrophe that occurred in New Orleans in 2005. Over 1,800 people were killed and over 500,000 were left without food, water and electricity. Who can forget the Superdome and its crowdedness that ultimately resulted in a situation that was morally and ethically, wrong. Wild animals have been treated better than the people that endured this terrible tragedy. Many in the African American community were very critical of President Bush 43rd because he failed to

13

act as quickly as he needed to in order to address the dire situation in New Orleans.

In fact, some with me being one of them, continue to believe that had most of the people been White rather than African American, President Bush would have responded with assistance more quickly. Also, the question still remains as to why something wasn't done early to ward off any issues that would cause failure of the levee. Things might have still gone awry and the levee might have still failed, but it was a well-known fact that this levee was not stable.

That's why it boggles my mind why so many in the Republican Party continue to say that President Obama is inept and lack the experience for the job. And I am bowled over by the fact that so many people have spent tremendous time, money and energy trying to disprove the fact that Barack Obama was born in the United States.

He has been called a communist and everything under the sun because he has chosen to do things the way he believed they should be done. But wait…Isn't that the reason why we voted for him in the first place? If we had wanted someone, who would follow and do what everyone expected or wanted him to do, I can assure you…There would be people complaining about this as well. That being said, like many Americans, there have been times when I've felt disillusioned and fed up with both the Democratic and the

Republican parties and I've often wondered why I even bother to vote. That feeling doesn't last long because I'm quickly reminded of the many great Americans who fought for the right to vote for African Americans and women.

The list is long of these great warriors who stood up and spoke up when it wasn't safe or popular to do so. These were troubling times and the country and the world were greatly divided.

Therefore, it would be a travesty to let all of their hard work and fight for equal justice to be all in vain. It is incumbent upon each one of us to carry the torch forward and instead of complaining about our dissatisfaction about the state of America and the President; it's incumbent upon me and everyone to do something to bring about change and to make a positive impact in the world. I and no one can be responsible for the behavior and acts of others no matter their political persuasion, but we can be part of the solution rather than the problem.

President John F. Kennedy said it best, "Ask Not What Your Country Can Do for You, Ask What You Can Do for Your Country."

CHAPTER THREE

Barack Obama - Under Fire
By Some in the
African American Community

Since the very beginning of Barack Obama's term as President of the United States, there have been Democrats who have openly supported him. This has been particularly true in the African American community. Too, a great many people who originally voted for President Obama have been amongst others who continue to vehemently denounce some of the decisions he has made on a variety of issues. Most notably of these critics have been Tavis Smiley and Dr. Cornell West. Tavis Smiley of CNN's Talk Live is a political commentator and he has made numerous appearances on political discussion shows such as MSNBC, ABC, and CNN. Dr. Cornell West is a frequent media commentator on political and social issues and has often appeared on CNN, C-SPAN, MSNBC, Fox News, PBS and programs such as Real Time With Bill Maher, The Colbert Report, and The Late Late Show With Craig Ferguson. Dr. West has held a number of high profile positions including Professorships at Yale, Princeton, Harvard and the University of Paris.

Both Tavis Smiley and Dr. West believe that African Americans haven't fared as well economically under President Obama. And they have made their feelings known on various levels.

There have been other critics who were instrumental in getting African Americans out to vote for President Barack Obama, but later felt much trepidation about their original support of him and many felt let down. Essentially, there's a feeling among many that the President has been more focused on implementing immigration policies and addressing the question of whether or not gays should have the right to marry along with other issues rather than issues in the African American community. This has no doubt raised a lot of troubling issues and concerns for the President, but at the end of the day,

President Obama couldn't afford to focus on one group of people because more than one group had a role in securing his election to the Office of President and more than one group of people make up the United States of America.

Though it may have appeared that President Obama was not moving fast enough to address a variety of African American issues, I personally believe that regardless of his actions, one or more groups will continue to be dissatisfied with his policies and his overall job performance.

For example, a great number of Americans continue to be disillusioned and dissatisfied with the way the President handled the health care initiative; the economy, including the near collapse of the automotive, banking and mortgage industry; lack of jobs that resulted in mast unemployment, including an overwhelming reliance on Americans need for unemployment benefits; the gay rights issues relative to the right to marry; immigration reform; the veteran administration travesty; the war, the fair trade initiative and other issues.

President Obama has been accused of causing all these issues to occur, but most of these issues were already occurring and inherited from the previous administration by President Obama.

To put it bluntly, these issues had already gotten out of control under President Bush 43rd and came to a crescendo when Barack Obama took office. But in fairness, the blame for these issues cannot all be laid at President Bush's door either because it took a long time for things to get as bad as they did in the economy and both parties share equal blame for the decline in our economy and related issues despite their overall accomplishments.

What has been really difficult and appalling for me to watch is the outrageous disrespect that has been shown for the Office of the President since Barack Obama has been President. In fact, I was so upset at one point that I took pen to paper and wrote to President Obama to express my dismay with many in the Republican Party and their treatment of him.

I essentially told President Obama to keep persevering and I said, "Don't let happen to you what I allowed to happen to me." I said this because in a previous job, I had allowed a bully to belittle my job performance and my qualifications and in a twisted way, for a time, I didn't perform at the high level I had been accustomed to. For seven consecutive years, I had been rated outstanding and all of a sudden under this new bully, I was not qualified to do my job.

Ultimately, in order to regain my footing, I decided that after 26 years in this company, I no longer recognized myself and I didn't like it. Therefore, I subsequently, resigned from the company.

However, in my case, the bad treatment of me occurred through subtle actions and then ramped up when I failed to kowtow and bow down to my bully who used a few weak Directors and direct reports to do her dirty work.

As a result, I felt a keen connection and identified greatly with what I saw occurring with President Obama and I didn't want to see him cave in to all that was going on and being said about him.

Primarily, it was difficult for me to have a front seat to all the crazy and unwarranted rhetoric that was being tossed about by many so called political pundits in the news and by others in the Republican Party and yes, some in the Democratic Party and say or do nothing to support President Obama. Though I wasn't expecting any type of response from him, a few weeks later I would receive a letter from the Office of the President thanking me for my support. From my standpoint, no sane person can look at all the crazy actions and hatred spewed towards him, including the constant veto and impeachment threats made by the Republican Party and not see blatant disrespect and in some cases, outright racism.

But when Barack Obama was first elected to the Office of President, many Whites were rallying around him and claiming him as more White than African American and African Americans were calling him a "Brotha." Some African Americans have had lots of chuckles about his obvious swagger and call him "cool." He definitely has a strong and demanding presence that I see as confidence and that's attractive in any man or woman.

The bottom-line is that people are always in a hurry to throw their arms around you when things are new and things are going well, but the minute things don't go the way they think they should, some people will take off running for the hills and do whatever they can to bring you down and distance themselves from you.

CHAPTER FOUR

My Early Memories
of the Office of President

I was nine year old when I first became aware that there was a President of the United States, but I really didn't understand too much about the role of the President. I only knew that at the time, Dwight Eisenhower was the President and that's it.

The fact that he was a Republican President went unnoticed by me because I didn't understand the process of electing a President and I certainly had no knowledge of the differences that existed between the Democratic and Republican Parties. If anything about the two political parties or the Presidency was discussed in school, and I'm sure that it was, it wasn't at a level that made any impact or had any significance in my young life. What I did understand and was aware of is the fact that my mother often worked very hard as a maid in White homes, scrubbing floors on her knees and washing their clothes using a wooden washboard, a tub of water and Oxford soap.

We would often receive used clothing and leftover food and money from them and particularly the Webb sisters. The Webb sisters were very well off and live in a large white and green house that appeared to have many rooms. I don't know because when I was required to pick up something from them, I could only go to the back of the house and knock on the door.

A hand would come out with a brown paper bag of goodies, but I never saw the face of the person that was giving the bag to me. This was just a sign of the times. We had full bellies and understood that we were loved and cared for and nothing else mattered to us.

In fact, I wasn't aware that we were really poor because our basic needs were being fully met. But this is the mind of an innocent nine years old African American girl who hadn't formed any biases or prejudices because we weren't brought up that way. In my case, I never saw any other races, but Whites in Mobile, Alabama and though the two races were separate, at the time, I didn't really understand all that it meant to be separate. I knew about separate waiting rooms, separate drinking fountains and riding in the back of the bus, but you can't question what you don't find odd, so I didn't find that unusual because it was all I had known.

I credit my mother for giving me the gift of not knowing there was a difference in our treatment because had I fully understood the reason for segregation, I don't believe I would be the well-grounded person that I am today. I truly believe that in some cases, ignorance is bliss.

As I've read and gathered research on our Presidents and their individual role in Civil Rights, I learned that Dwight D. Eisenhower was a big supporter of Civil Rights and in fact, though Truman had begun the process of desegregation in the Armed Forces, it was President Eisenhower who would do more to make it happen.

In his first State of the Union address in February 1953, Dwight D. Eisenhower's said the following: "I propose to use whatever authority that exists in the office of the President to end segregation in the District of Columbia, including the Federal Government, and any segregation in the Armed Forces." This announcement and affirmation caused President Eisenhower to be confronted with great opposition, but he used government control of military spending to force the change, stating "Wherever Federal

Funds are expended; I do not see how any American can justify… a discrimination in the expenditure of those funds".

He also sent Federal Armed Forces to Little Rock, Arkansas to enforce desegregation in schools and protected the right to vote.

As an eighth grader, I became fully aware that John F. Kennedy was the President of the United States and his assassination affected me in a way that I never imagined because I didn't realize that I cared so much.

This is not meant to be a derogatory or disrespectful statement…What I mean by this is that prior to President Kennedy's assassination, I had only known about the death of a relative or friend and their deaths were mostly attributed to age related and natural occurrences or diseases. The only exception is my infant baby brother, Jerome who died from unknown causes at six months of age and that was very painful for me and my family. I can remember it as though it was yesterday. A loud scream came from my parent's bedroom which also served as our living room during the day. I ran quickly to see what was going on. My mother was crying because my brother who was lying next to her in the bed had died. I can recall going to the hospital, but little else other than the long trek down the dusty road leading to his burial site.

The following days leave me with a blur except that for a long time thereafter, my mother continued to have difficulty accepting my brother's death and it would be a long time before she would be back to herself and the mother I had known prior to my infant brother's death.

Because President Kennedy's death and the aftermath of it was played over and over again on television, the feeling of sorrow that I experienced will forever be delineated in my mind.

I can remember it as though it was just yesterday. Everyone in our class cried and became weary and stunned to silence. Some of the student's heads fell to their desks in tremendous anguish and sorrow.

I suspect they were shedding tears and didn't want to share this moment with anyone. It wasn't that we knew so much about what President Kenney had done for the Country but here was a good looking and as far as we knew a good human being. But even that was not the reason for our grief and I believe we didn't really know or understood why we had been so grief stricken. In the coming days, I would find myself along with the rest of my family glued to the television set watching the same horrible event unfold over and over again in front of our eyes.

If things weren't bad enough, there would come the terrible day when everyone would get a glimpse of President Kennedy's murderer, Lee Harvey Oswald.

As we watched to see the man that had committed such a terrible crime, we weren't prepared for the next thing that followed. Jack Ruby, a nightclub operator stepped forward and shot Lee Harvey Oswald dead. I can remember thinking to myself, "What is going on?" But I still didn't understand enough about all of this to really grasp all my feelings about it.

As days passed, I found myself very engrossed in everything and anything to do with the Kennedy family and I desired to know what was going on in their personal lives, including how they were getting along after the death of our 35th President of the United States, John F. Kennedy. I was so proud of how Jacqueline Kennedy had handled herself throughout the funeral and the years after as well and I admired Caroline and her brother, John, John and was grief stricken again by the untimely death of John Kennedy, Jr. I guess you might say, it was because of this family that I paid more attention to Lyndon B. Johnson and closely watched everything that was going on in his Presidency and his family life including his daughters and of course, Lady Bird. Who could not be interested in someone name Lady Bird.

From that point on, I tried to watch all the Presidential inaugurations and I was interested in some Presidents more than others. I was particularly fond of Jimmy Carter, Bill Clinton and George Bush III but others would go practically unnoticed by me.

For example, when Richard Nixon resigned from the Presidency due to Watergate, I really didn't understand the entire ramifications and I didn't understand what all the fuss was about; however, I would later learn that the fuss was about an incident that had occurred during the 1972 U.S. Presidential campaign where a group of agents employed by the re-election organization of President Richard Nixon were caught breaking into the Democratic Party headquarters in the Watergate building, Washington, DC.

The problem was made worse by attempts to conceal the fact that senior White House officials had approved the burglary, and eventually forced the resignation of President Nixon Mostly, what I've learned from all the Presidents over the years is that they're human with the same human frailties that we all have. No one is perfect and it's so important for us to keep that in mind regardless of one's political preference.

CHAPTER FIVE

The Early Years
of our Political Parties

Looking back to the beginning of our country's political parties, I found that the first party convention took place in Jackson, Michigan, on July 6, 1854. This was the party of Thomas Jefferson and it later became the Democratic Party.

But it was a protest in Ripon, Wisconsin that resulted in The Republican Party. There was a meeting held on February 28,1854 with the Free Soilers, a group of anti-slavery activists who met to start a new grassroots movement. This movement was embraced at various times by Martin Van Buren, a Democrat, who ran unsuccessfully for the presidency on the Free Soiler Party ticket in 1848, and David Wilmot, a member of the U.S. House of Representatives from the years 1845-1851.

The Republican Party gained support because of disillusioned northern Whigs who were established in 1833 and are one of America's oldest political parties. Abraham Lincoln and four other U.S. Presidents were of the Whig Party.

The party was founded in opposition to the centralizing policies of President Andrew Jackson, a Democrat who worked hard to expand Executive power at the expense of Congress and favored the spoils system, also called the patronage system.

The patronage system is a practice in which a political party who wins an election rewards its campaign workers and other active supporters by appointing to government posts or other favors. Though some would deny it, we continue to have patronage going on today.

In addition to opposing autocratic rule and cronyism, American Whigs advocated economic development through domestic manufacturing, federally-subsidized infrastructure projects, a national bank, protective tariffs and public education. The collapse of the Whig Party in the 1850s resulted in the emergence of the Republican Party.

Three traditions caused the birth of the Republican Party.

- The Reform Tradition
- Economic Policies
- Nativism

The Reform Tradition

The reform tradition helped inspire many of those who opposed slavery's extension into the territories. The Liberty Party and the Free Soil Party were the driving force of this movement. Nearly all the Republican leaders except Abraham Lincoln had strong connections to some of these antebellum reform movements.

Economic Policies

The economic policies were introduced by Henry Clay and others in the Whig Party. He believed that the government should develop the American economy by promoting protective tariffs on textile and iron industries.

The protective tariffs paid for internal improvements for transportation infrastructure that include roads, rivers, harbors, and railroads.

Nativism

Many Americans worked hard to define a national identity, rather than bending to ideas or institutions. John Jay believed that only Protestants were good Americans. The Irish and Germans were mostly Catholic so many Protestants believe that the American institutions would be taken over by illiterate paupers with an allegiance to the Vatican.

Though there had been other Republican Presidents, prior to Abraham Lincoln, he was the first to be voted in by the people under the Constitution of the United States. Abraham Lincoln did a lot to forge freedom of the slaves, but his untimely death due to his assassination by John Wilkes Booth ended and halted the work that he was doing in this area. However, later there would be others in the Republican and Democratic Party to pick up the banner and move the country forward.

The Democratic Party grew out of the Republican Democratic Party and in the early years, the party was more focused on Whites in particular farmers and agricultural issues while the Republican Party was the party of African Americans. The Democratic Party controlled all the southern states and eventually captured a large part of the Northern States. The Democratic Party didn't support Civil Rights as opposed to the Republican Party and they did everything they could to keep from approving legislation for Civil Rights. However, it was Lyndon B. Johnson's desire and approval of the Civil Rights Act of 1964 that led a great number of African Americans to pledge their allegiance to the Democratic Party.

George Washington and John Adams are the only Presidents who were elected to the Office of President outside of the Constitution of the United States. George Washington was an Independent but affiliated with the Federalist Party and John Adams was also a member of the Federalist Party. He was against owning slaves and never owned any.

CHAPTER SIX

Early Roles of African Americans in the Republican Party, Early Parties and Presidents

More than 100 years ago, the Republican Party was the party of older African Americans. This was greatly attributed to the fact that this party supported freedom of the slaves and other civil liberties. However, when Barry Goldwater, a Republican, was elected Senator of Arizona, he believed strongly that Civil Rights were unconstitutional and he believed that the government shouldn't have a say in how each state dealt with Civil Rights and that each state should exist without interference from any other person, government or entity. Needless to say, Barry Goldwater's beliefs and denouncement of Civil Rights didn't sit well in the African American community.

However, a different strategy was for African Americans to have an even stronger say and representation in the Republican Party while running for a variety of offices and being elected to these offices.

In these roles, Hiram Revels, Benjamin Turner, Robert De Large, Josiah Wells and Jefferson Long were able to help their fellow African American live better lives. However, the Southern States reacted by making the lives of African Americans more difficult. The following pages will introduce you to these great men and their roles in politics and the community they represented.

HIRAM REVELS

Born to free parents in North Carolina, Hiram Revels was a freed man his entire life and the first African American to serve in the U.S. Congress.

BENJAMIN S. TURNER

Benjamin S. Turner grew up as a slave with no formal education. He was in the House of Representatives for the state of Alabama and he was a wealthy real estate owner.

ROBERT C. DE LARGE

Robert C. De Large was in the House of Representatives for South Carolina. His parents were free and considered to be of the mulatto elite. De Large parents were also slaveholders and his father was a tailor while his mother was a seamstress.

De Large was considered to be an elite African American because he was a member of the Brown Fellowship Society, a group of expert artisans who led people of color.

JOSIAH WALLS

Josiah Walls was born a slave but became Florida's first African American Congressman. He is the only African American to be unseated three times despite the many controversies that surrounded him.

JEFFERSON LONG

Jefferson Long was born a slave and later became the first African American to speak in Georgia's House of Congress. He was a tailor, politician, storekeeper and educator.

JOSEPH RAINEY

Born a slave, Joseph Rainey was the first African American to serve in the U.S. House of Representatives.

ROBERT ELLIOTT

Robert Elliott established a law practice and was instrumental in helping to develop the local Republican Party and served in the state constitutional convention. He was also the first African-American commanding general of the South Carolina National Guard and had a role in the formation of a militia to fight the Ku Klux Klan.

These were extremely difficult times, yet, each one of the African American Senators and Representatives were able to carve out good lives for themselves while working hard to enrich the lives of others. Some of them grew to great heights despite the adversities they faced. It would seem to me that if these men could do so much with much less than we have today in terms of freedom, technology and other advancements, then I have a hard time wrapping my mind around why we still continue to fight racial imbalances and justice for all Americans.

Today, many in the African American community, believe that the Republican Party only cares about the betterment of White America. I once believed this as well, but I've come to realize and appreciate the importance of having African American representation in both the Democratic and Republican Party. It just makes good sense.

In fact, there are a number of high profile African Americans that are members of the Republican Party. This only assures that the interests and rights of African Americans and other people of color are protected. As a young woman, I can recall my mother being so frustrated with both parties that at one point, she was filled with disgust. Later she indicated to me that she didn't care who was in the White House because, she said, "Most of what's being implemented will benefit African Americans as well, even though that might not be the intention." Though I didn't quite understand what she meant by this statement at the time, I later came to realize that she was right.

There are some issues and initiatives that do not fall within any type of racial or special interest group category and will benefit all races of people regardless of their voting preferences.

That being said, I personally believe that it is very important to vote for a candidate that you fully support because you need to feel and believe that your candidate of choice has your best interest at heart. It's not wise to simply jump on the band wagon with people who look like you.

More importantly, you need to understand the issues and the consequences of not having a voice in the different issues that come before you in the form of a ballot.

Though I've voted Democratic all of my life, I've learned that many of our younger African Americans are more open minded and willing to look at all the facts about all parties before giving their votes to particular candidates or parties. In fact, you may be surprised to learn that some of our past Presidents who were admired for their support of Civil Rights and liberties were actually members of the Republican Party. The following pages list the names of our past and more current Presidents and their Party affiliations.

REPUBLICAN PRESIDENTS

1.   Abraham Lincoln (1861–1865)
2.   Ulysses S. Grant (1869–1877)
3.   Rutherford B. Hayes (1877–1881)
4.   James A. Garfield (1881)
5.   Chester A. Arthur (1881–1885)
6.   Benjamin Harrison (1889–1893)
7.   William McKinley (1897–1901)
8.   Theodore Roosevelt (1901–1909)
9.   William Howard Taft (1909–1913)
10. Warren G. Harding (1921–1923)
11. Calvin Coolidge (1923–1929)
12. Herbert Hoover (1929–1933)
13. Dwight D. Eisenhower (1953–1961)
14. Richard Nixon (1969–1974)
15. Gerald Ford (1974–1977)
16. Ronald Reagan (1981–1989)
17. George H. W. Bush (1989–1993)
18. George W. Bush (2001–2009)

DEMOCRATIC PRESIDENTS

1. Andrew Jackson (1829–1837)
2. Martin Van Buren (1837–1841)
3. James K. Polk (1845–1849)
4. Franklin Pierce (1853–1857)
5. James Buchanan (1857–1861)
6. Andrew Johnson (1865-1869)
7. Grover Cleveland (1885–1889), (1893–1897)
8. Woodrow Wilson (1913–1921)
9. Franklin D. Roosevelt (1933–1945)
10. Harry S. Truman (1945–1953)
11. John F. Kennedy (1961–1963)
12. Lyndon B. Johnson (1963–1969)
13. Jimmy Carter (1977–1981)
14. Bill Clinton (1993–2001)
15. Barack H. Obama (2008–2016)

DEMOCRATIC-REPUBLICAN PRESIDENT

1.   Thomas Jefferson (1801–1809)
2.   James Madison (1809–1817)
3.   James Monroe (1817–1825)
4.   John Quincy Adams (1825–1829)

WHIG PARTY

1.   William Henry Harrison (1841)
2.   John Tyler (1841–1845)
3.   Zachary Taylor (1849–1850)
4.   Millard Fillmore (1850–1853)

NATIONAL REPUBLICAN PARTY

John Quincy Adams (1825–1829) was the president when the Democratic-Republican Party split. He led the National Republicans (Anti-Jacksonians) along with Henry Clay (who later founded the Whig Party).

INDEPENDENT PARTY

1.   George Washington (1789–1797)
2.   John Tyler (1841–1845)

NATIONAL UNION PARTY

1.   Abraham Lincoln (1865)
2.   Andrew Johnson (1865–1868)

CHAPTER SEVEN

Accomplishments and Failures

When Barack Obama announced his candidacy for President of the United States, I personally, believed that he had little chance of winning and as I addressed in my book, "On the Shoulders of Greatness," he wasn't my original choice for President. I was and continue to be a big supporter of Hillary Clinton because I believe she is a strong, extremely qualified and extraordinary woman.

Her strengths and capabilities have been reflected in so many levels in both her personal life and in her political career. However; as time passed, I came to realize the significance of voting for Barack Obama not only from a historical point of view, but he appeared to be the right choice and the catalyst we needed to unite the country and both parties. His failure to unite the country and the Democratic and Republican Party isn't completely his fault. The reality is that change can't occur if the people you're trying to unite are continually setting up barriers. People have to be willing to participate in constructive dialogue for changes and improvements to occur.

I don't believe that President Obama envisioned that he would be confronted with so much opposition as he has seen as President of the United States. However, I believe that early on, President Barack Obama made a series of errors in judgments in his cabinet choices and his picks for advisors and it nearly derailed his Presidency.

This included the financial advisers that he chose to assist him at the beginning of his term in key areas; e.g. the accountants and financial advisors, his choice to elect several of his close friends to his cabinet and the selection of Joe Biden as his Vice President.

First of all, when you are choosing advisers and I can say this because I've been a consultant for the last ten years, it's important to keep them truly in an advisory role that doesn't appear to over-lap into a decision making role. This is particularly important for areas where financial advisement is required.

It's like putting the fox in the hen house and we all know what happens in that scenario. Also, you should keep your work and friends separate even if you have a position that you believe can be performed well by a close friend, I believe that more often than not the choice to hire them will backfire on you.

There will inevitably be times when the friends will make mistakes that will be no different from someone who isn't a friend, but yet, your friends will be judged more harshly because of the relationship you have with them. This happened with the White House Social Secretary position that was held by Desiree Rogers, a good friend of the Obamas and in particular Michele Obama.

When the party crashers were able to penetrate an important event with various dignitaries in attendance, it was seen as a huge security risk on all fronts and badly reflected on President Obama's choice for the position. Particularly, since Desiree Rogers stated that she had ensured that every entrance was covered, including the entrance for people who weren't on the list of attendees.

It was later discovered that Desiree Rogers didn't follow the usual protocol to ensure adequate coverage and security assurance and she was allowed to voluntarily resign from the position. Though everything turned out fine at the event, someone had to be the scapegoat and unfortunately, it was Desiree Rogers.

The Attorney General Eric Holder is a very close friend of Barack Obama and they share similar life experiences because they both grew up middle class and are the sons of immigrant fathers.

But Eric Holder has admitted that he and Barack Obama don't share the typical African American experience. Eric Holder resigned from his position in 2014, but before resigning, he was very outspoken and candid about critical issues including the death of Trayvon Martin. He also wasn't shy in advocating a variety of Civil Rights issues.

The respect that President Obama and Eric Holder have for one another continues to be stronger than any controversies that arose due to Eric Holder's actions. President Obama plain and simply supported Eric Holder throughout his Attorney General tenure and both men understood well that the other had his back. Therefore, whenever there have been issues about something Eric Holder had said or done, the President didn't feel it necessary to explain it away. He simply allowed Eric Holder to do the job that he elected him for and that's the way it should have been because if you have to always be looking for ways to explain away what someone in your cabinet is doing...then that's a problem.

But the appointment of Vice President Joe Biden was a greater concern for me. Let me be clear, I've always enjoyed

Joe Biden's frankness as a Senator and Senior member of Congress. And when Biden was a Senator, I would wait with great anticipation to see what he would have to say about prospective appointments that were coming before the Senate for approval.

Biden has a no holds barred, in your face way of grilling appointments to get at the truth to the questions he asks. However, I was troubled by the appointment mostly, because of Barack Obama's and Joe Biden's bitter and often confrontational Presidential debates. How can you have such intense feeling about a person's lack of knowledge, experience and qualifications when it comes to the war and foreign policy and yet, set on the sideline and not feel that you are better suited and qualified for the job?

Though I realize that this type of rhetoric is a part of politics, I also know it's difficult to have such a critical position as the Vice President of the United States held by someone who really feels that they are the best candidate for the lead job, in this case, the job of the President of the United States. I know because I've held positions where some of the people on my team were more knowledgeable in certain areas, but it takes more than having knowledge to get the job done. You have to be able to provide the direction and strategies necessary to achieve the desired outcome rather than simply getting tasks done. I sometimes wonder how much Biden has been in Obama's ear, trying to tell him what he should or shouldn't do.

Mostly, I wonder what Biden truly thinks about Barack Obama's performance as President. Is he second guessing him or is he really as supportive as he appears to be? I don't know, but I do know that all the talk about the possibility of Joe Biden running for President in 2016 gives me pause to ponder and question what's really going on behind the scene.

However, the Biden's and the Obama's appear to genuinely like and respect one another, so at the end of the day, that's all that matters. In every Presidential Administration, there are always issues and challenges. The next few pages cover some of the key challenges faced by Barack Obama along with initiatives and accomplishments that have had positive outcomes.

The Economy

The economy is dependent upon two variables, supply and demand and how well the needs are being met for each element such as the job market, the oil industry, banking and mortgage, automotive industry and other key indicators.

Each industry, however, must be robust enough to sustain and guard against financial ruin or collapse of the industry. This all depends on how well each industry is managing its finances, resources and overall business. If either supply or demand is out of sync the economy will take a hit. Under Obama's watch, the economy suffered greatly, but it's important to note that this wasn't an overnight decline.

The decline in the economy began long before Barack Obama became President. But there was so much focus on the war, terror groups and other catastrophes during the previous Administration, problems in the economy appeared to go unnoticed. This is not to say that there shouldn't have been focusing on other issues. What I'm saying is that you have to be watching everything closely and managing the things that appear to be simmering but are really close to blowing up.

The simple truth is…there is generally a timeframe when you have enough information to know that if you don't do something and act rapidly, you'll end up with a powder cake and in this case, a doom and gloom situation and that's exactly what happened in the case of the economy.

Every facet of the economy was adversely affected and suffered its own disaster and it would take nearly four years of President Obama's first term to restore the economy to some sort of normalcy. Some would argue that it actually took longer and there continues to be more work to be done in this area.

The Jobs Market and Unemployment

While I was continuing to see plenty of vacant jobs on different job boards, the unemployment roll was getting larger and larger and people were becoming maxed out in their unemployment benefits.

Though there were numerous extensions made by the government, the need for unemployment benefits by so many Americans was astronomical. In fact, very talented and professional people lost jobs due to downsizing and found themselves in need of financial assistance. It has certainly gotten a lot better, but jobs are still hard to obtain.

This is greatly attributed to stiffer competition as well as hiring and qualification standards required by companies. Today, many companies rely more and more on recruiters to do pre-screening for job vacancies. The thought is that the use of recruiters saves employers time by doing most of the upfront work involved in the selection of viable candidates.

Generally, this includes sifting through a robust applicant database to extract the name and resumes of candidates that closely match the employer's hiring criteria. Recruiters also hold interviews with prospective candidates to determine next steps.

Sometimes, the interview and selection process has little to do with your actual job skills and more to do with matching a particular personality type to a job and/or work site.

However, it has been my observation that a great number of the recruiters have little knowledge of the actual job for which they are doing pre-screening, or in some cases, they appear to be looking for people with lots of experience. The problem with this is that simply having the experience isn't enough and doesn't necessarily equate to the best person for the job.

The Automotive Manufacturing Industry Bail Out

The Automotive Manufacturing Industry nearly became a debacle because of poor management decisions by Chrysler, Ford and General Motors.

Though tied to the Energy Crisis that began in 2003 - 2008, these companies struggled because they had concentrated their efforts on producing high gas guzzlers such as trucks and sports utility vehicles because they resulted in higher profit margins for them.

But the increase in the cost of fuel forced them to produce more energy efficient vehicles. However, this was difficult to do because they were already experiencing losses due to the declining purchase of the larger vehicles and requests for more efficient use vehicles.

I personally, was so infuriated and frustrated with the Automotive Industry that I developed an action plan and mailed it to each company and offered my consulting services. I provided them with actual details on what they needed to do to turn their companies around. I only heard back from Chrysler who told me thank you but they didn't need my services; however, they along with the other companies implemented many of the ideas that I suggested.

Coincidental, I don't believe so. I believe the companies may have had some of the ideas that I suggested on their radar, but my question is…If this is the case, why didn't they implement the actions I outlined prior to needing a bailout? I suggested closing plants that they had in other countries because it didn't make sense to continue to have them if they weren't manufacturing vehicles and losing profits. I suggested that people be able to design their own cars online and that a deposit be taken for each car so that no money is lost in the design only to have people change their mind about purchasing a vehicle from them. I also suggested making cars that were cost effective such as smaller compact cars that could get higher gas mileage and most importantly, I suggested that they talk with the folks closest to the work, the employees.

My point was that employees knew where the inefficiencies were and could help in finding solutions to their financial problems as well as identify problems in their processes. No one ever mentioned the letter from Beverly Montgomery but I knew it was sent and received by all of them. In the final analysis, I along with others was highly upset when President Obama decided to bail the automotive companies out of the hole they had dug for themselves. But the actual plan to do a bail out occurred in President Bush Administration.

Essentially, President Obama decided to act on what had already been agreed upon and decided on by President Bush. I guess the flip side of the coin is that President Obama could have done nothing and the economy and the automotive industry would have suffered even greater losses.

The Banking and Mortgage Industry

Banks are notorious for imposing all types of fees on their customers. They think nothing of charging late fees and all types of banking charges and yet, they were in need of a bail out. Granted they paid the money back to the government, but it still left a bitter taste in many Americans mouths because Who was bailing us out of our financial woes?

Nevertheless, we can't do without the banking industry because it crosses and touches every fabric of our daily lives. The Mortgage Industry practically bulldozed their way into Americans lives, promising that they could qualify them for ridiculously expensive home loans and houses that were priced far out of most Americans financial realms.

Loan agents went as far as to help people qualify using unscrupulous tactics knowing full well that the customers probably wouldn't be able to sustain their payments for the homes once they got in them. A great many of hard working Americans not only lost their homes, but they also had nowhere to go. This greed of the industry caused many families to break up and some ended up homeless and on the streets while the Mortgage Industry was handed a slap on the wrist and again, a bailout from their problems.

Much improvement has occurred and there have been several plans implemented to help those who are underwater in their homes or near the brink of losing them. But even with that many Americans continues to struggle with their mortgage payments.

For example, the implementation of more rigorous qualification criteria has been put in place to guard against defaults and other issues, but the plans implemented to alleviate some of the pain come with their own set of problems.

If you don't have a good credit score you don't qualify for many of the plans and particularly, if you desire to take money out of your home via equity, even a small amount of money. It doesn't matter if you have never been late on your mortgage payments so there continues to be a lot of work necessary in this area.

Healthcare Initiative

The Healthcare Initiative is definitely great in theory, but it also appears to punish people who can't afford to pay for health care even with the support of the government. It was initially plagued with a lot of problems, but this is to be expected with the rollout of any plan and system.

The bottom-line is that most Americans and eventually all Americans will have some type of health care plan. But I don't believe that people should be punished on their taxes for not having a healthcare plan. This is pouring salt in the wound because some if not most, people rely on every dollar they get back from their tax refund to pay some type of bill or debt.

There needs to be another way to encourage people to take a more proactive role in their health care. The problem is some people don't make much money on their jobs, and yet, their employers are offering them plans at nearly $300 or more per month. This is not reasonable for someone who barely makes $10 an hour.

The Oil Industry

I'm convinced that the Oil Industry is being controlled by a group of crooks who like to yank our chain by imposing high prices on oil at every turn. Then when they have sucked and squeezed every cent out of us, all of a sudden the crooks will have a decreased of a few pennies reflected at the gas pumps.

Nevertheless, we have to have fuel for our automobiles so we are held hostage by those who are making billions of dollars in oil industry and doing very little to lessen the drain on our wallets.

Essentially, we are being held hostage by those who we depend on to provide us with oil for fuel for our automobiles and other usage. I wrongly believed that the United States depended greatly on oil from other countries, but the simple fact is that 40% of oil used in our country for fuel is produced by the United States.

Our remaining needs for oil are met by Canada, Saudi Arabia, Mexico, Venezuela and Nigeria. This begs the question…Why can't more cost controls be placed on oil producers in the United States? I don't believe they have any incentives to change because the oil producers are not suffering the way average Americans suffer at the gas pumps.

Gays and Lesbians Right to Marry

On June 26, 2015, the Supreme Court ruled that Gays and Lesbians have the right to marry. It further stated that gays and lesbians who are currently married shall have their marriages recognized in all states throughout the Country.

Therefore, along with the 36 states that currently allow gays and lesbians to be married, the remaining 16 states are required to immediately allow gays and lesbians to be married in these states as well.

For me, this has been a no brainer issue. Although I grew up in a Baptist Church with strong beliefs that marriage should be between a man and a woman, I grew to believe that if gays and lesbians desired to marry, it was their right and their business.

Years ago, I had a boss, who happened to be a gay man. He was the best boss that I've ever had and I learned a lot from him. I believe without a discussion on the subject, he taught me to be sensitive to others and to stay in my lane. He died in the 80s' from AIDS, but I know he would be thrilled about the right to marry the one you love.

Particularly, since he could never talk about his significant other and when he was stricken with AIDS, he suffered greatly because he didn't have the medical coverage that he needed and of course, AIDS was fairly new and we didn't know as much about it as we do today.

He was treated very badly on the job and at one time, it was necessary for him to return to work because his sick leave benefits were depleted and he could no longer remain home. I can recall seeing him lie on the floor at work because he was so ill.

Ultimately, he was forced to be hospitalized where he died. I can't help but think that if he had been allowed to marry, he wouldn't have had an issue with depleted benefits because he could have been aided by spousal benefits. And this would have possibly extended his life. I would love to say to him…It's been a long fight and struggle of many but look how far we've come, Mort…Look how far we've come!

Pacific Rim Trade Deal

Years ago, I had several people on my team who desired to have someone other than myself in my management position. I told them that it was not important for them to like me, but it was important for them to respect me and support my efforts for the good of the department. I further stated that if they couldn't do so, then I could help them get out the department and go where they could be happy.

The bottom-line is that I wasn't about to let them hurt my chances nor the stability and success of the department. I say that to say that when Nancy Pelosi and several members of the Democratic Party went against Barack Obama on the passage of the Pacific Rim Trade Bill, it infuriated me. It would give Obama the authority to negotiate a 12-country Pacific Rim trade deal.

However, omitted from the legislation is Trade Adjustment Assistance, a program that provides aid and job training for workers who lose their jobs to trade. I can understand Democrats and others having a concern about workers losing their jobs or having jobs go out the country and the need for job training and aid.

But initially, Nancy Pelosi and other Democrats didn't appear to be looking at the big picture to see that a lot of jobs would be created as well. Also, they failed to recognize the other opportunities that this initiative would create, such as the ability to share and collaborate with other countries.

This is a big deal and important for a robust economy as well as it creates more trade options for the United States. However, later, with a thin margin, Democrats and Republicans voted to advance legislation to give President Obama fast-track authority to negotiate very large Pacific trade deals. In this area, the Republicans have been far more accepting of this bill than the Democrats so here again, you have people of the same party going against the President.

It is so disrespectful and I can't help but wonder what the President thinks about all of this dissenting from his own party.

CHAPTER EIGHT

The John Boehner Factor

In 2014, the Republican Party was able to become the Majority Party in the House and Senate because they were clever enough, to get their constituency stirred up about the economy, the bail outs and other key initiatives.

However, I do believe that a lot of Republican voters were fed up with the stalemate in Congress and blamed it on the Democrats who wouldn't fold to Republicans need to control. But I also believe that the constant rhetoric heard in the news daily with John Boehner and others in the Republican Party contributed greatly to their ability to get voters out to the polls to vote for Republican candidates and key positions particularly, those held by Democrats. That's exactly what happened and the rest is history. It doesn't take a brain surgeon to see what happened here.

From my standpoint, the Republicans capitalized on what they saw as strong arm tactics on the part of the President and they didn't like it.

But in reality, President Obama has been nothing but totally disrespected by many of the Republican Senators, Congressmen and women. John Boehner has been the most divisive House Speaker of all times.

He spews hatred and disdain for President Barack Obama and I don't feel bad about saying it. He single handedly has done more to cause a rift between the two parties than anyone in history.

If that's not bad enough, he and others in the Republican Party threatened the President with impeachment and filed a lawsuit against him because they didn't like the way he dealt with the health care initiative and the immigration issue.

Boehner and others have complained about nearly every initiative President Obama has desired to put forth for approval and threatened that they wouldn't approve most of the bills he authored.

It's a sad commentary when the President of the United States has to work under these types of hostile situations. It says a lot about where we are in the Country and that is very far apart. Though no one likes to talk about it, the case of race is up front and center in the threat of impeachment of President Obama and other issues in the United States.

CHAPTER NINE

The 2008 Primaries and Key Candidates

When John Edwards, who was holding himself up to be holier than thou was found to be having an ongoing affair with a woman who worked for him as a Graphic Designer, his behavior proved that you can rarely trust some politicians or take them at their word.

This was particularly bad because his wife was suffering with cancer and despite that fact; he was carrying on with another woman and fathered a child with her.

Though much of what happened played out in the media, I'm sure that we'll never know the real truth about how this terrible news negatively affected the health of his wife who stood so faithfully at his side during his campaign and throughout their marriage. As a woman, I felt her pain and have little respect for any woman who knowingly goes after a married man.

Though he initially denied the affair, he later was forced to admit it and acknowledge the child that he had fathered with his mistress. His bad behavior ended his chances of becoming President of the United States and holding any other office.

Barack Obama had his own set of problems when an old tape by his Pastor Jeremiah Wright came back to haunt him. It showed how Pastor Wright had made derogatory comments against Whites in one of his Sunday Sermons.

The discovery of this taped sermon, forced Barack Obama to distance himself from Jeremiah Wright and declare that he didn't hold the same views that were heard in the taped sermon. Some African Americans had problems with Barack Obama's dissent and obvious failure to really stand up for Reverend Wright.

Barack Obama indicated that it was a tough decision to remove himself from any relationship with Pastor Wright but his actions spoke louder than words. We have never heard anything more about Jeremiah Wright.

Hillary Clinton had both a liability and asset in her husband Bill Clinton. Though brilliant, his roving eye and the Monica Lewinski escapade in the White House was still in the forefront of people's minds.

Though it may not have been mentioned, people quietly talked about it behind closed doors. But Hillary was seen as an individual and separate and apart from Bill Clinton and his infidelity issues.

Her qualifications clearly outweighed any of the personal issues that she and her husband shared. At the end of the day, the Clintons are highly liked in the African American community and Bill Clinton's Presidency saw many accomplishments and some failures like the Healthcare Initiative.

But there was no love lost between the Clintons and Barack Obama. In fact, during the Clinton and Obama debates, it was clear that the Clintons didn't believe that Barack Obama was qualified for the Office of President. Barack Obama and Hillary's debates were often heated and angry in nature.

The other controversy occurred when John Mc Cain chose Sarah Palin for his choice as a Vice Presidential running mate. There are so many reasons why this was a bad idea, but I believe the fact that her daughter was pregnant and unmarried didn't set well with a lot of people in the

Republican Party. Also, Sarah Palin would later shoot herself in the foot when she made the statement that she could see Russia from her back yard. This was made in reference to a question about her foreign policy knowledge and her statement proved that she obviously had little if any, foreign policy knowledge.

Though I'm impressed with Mitt Romney's resilience and his "never give up spirit," I was dismayed that Mitt Romney foolishly believed that the African American vote could be bought.

To me this indicated that he believed that the African American vote was bought for Barack Obama. He foolishly remarked that African Americans were promised gifts if they voted for Obama. If that's the case, I want to know, "Where's my gift?" But seriously, African Americans voted for Barack Obama for the same reasons that most Americans voted for him, they were seeking hope.

There may have been some desire to have the first African American as a President, but that was only a fraction of why I voted for him.

I don't claim to speak for all African Americans, but I would say that we are much smarter and more open minded than to look simply one dimensional at a person or political figure. However, I feel that Mitt Romney could have won the Republican Primaries in 2011 if he had only shown himself to be more authentic. On television, he appeared to be unsteady and awfully uncomfortable in debates. His personality doesn't appear to be very confrontational and so, I believe this was a critical area that needed to be worked on and practiced with his team of advisors.

Clearly any person that can become a self-made millionaire has something to say. More importantly, this is the type of person that most people would want to see in the White House.

Many of the other candidates that were paraded before us went practically unnoticed by me. They didn't address my interest and as a result, I rarely listened too much of what they were saying including Rick Perry, who had that famous brain freeze when he couldn't remember the Department of Energy.

I've had this happen to me before, so I could relate to what he was feeling. For me, a brain freeze occurred after I had worked on an important presentation all day and because I wanted to make a great presentation, I also phoned my boss later that afternoon because I wanted to review the information with him and he never returned my phone message and it was all part of a set up. At the time, I was also in a very intense MBA program so I had a lot on my shoulders.

Nevertheless, I showed up at the meeting ready to deliver, but right away was shut down by a barrage of questions that I knew the answers but my brain shut down. I was unbelievably tired. But I made no apologies for my performance.

Things happen and I took responsibility for it and that was it. What more can you say...everyone has had some type of brain freeze moment and some are worse than others.

Therefore, I was not critical of Rick Perry's performance, but what turn me off were the constant character assassinations made about Barack Obama. It sickened me and still makes me cringe inside. But nothing gives me the cringe factor more than John Boehner. I just don't see where he gets the idea that he doesn't need to respect President Obama.

As I've watched several state of the union addresses made by President Obama, I couldn't help but notice the Republicans reactions to what President Obama was saying, but I particularly have noticed how much John Boehner has an intense dislike for the President. He can't cover it up. It's almost as though he has something to prove to the other fellow Republicans.

Whatever the case, I believe that he is a poor Representative for the Republican Party, and though they may have won the House and Senate majority, the Republicans lose in the tact, sensitivity and respect department.

CHAPTER TEN

2016 Election and Candidates

As I write this book, Democratic and Republican candidates are getting in position to run for the President of the United States in 2016. Hillary Clinton was the first Democrat to throw her hat in the ring and right away the Republican Party began attacking her for using her personal email and business email together.

They also more than insinuated that she had deleted some of the emails from the server she had at her home and accused her of lying about it. However, whether she did or didn't delete some of her emails is irrelevant to me because most, if not all politicians lie in one form or another to protect their interest. That's just a fact! I know some of you will raise your eyebrows and say, I can't believe she said that…well, I did and I mean it. In Hillary's position, I don't believe I would have turned all my emails over to anyone. I can remember coming in late to my job one day and found that my computer had been hijacked by the compliance and auditing department.

I was given some lie about someone had gone to the press and put out bad or negative information about the company and I was told that I and a few others were thought to be among the culprits.

At the time, I can recall feeling a tremendous invasion of privacy and I didn't believe I had done anything to raise any suspicion about me. However, it took me ten years, after leaving the company, to figure out that I was told a lie and that I was in fact, being investigated.

Why? Well, it all goes back to the bully and others who resented the fact that I had been very successful in leading my groups, despite the many consultants that the bully brought in to say the contrary.

Simply put, when people are against you, you have to do whatever and use whatever necessary to protect yourself and your rights. That's why I admire Hillary Clinton. She doesn't take any crap and she sticks to her guns and I say BRAVO to her. As far as I can see, the country will be in great hands with her at the helm as President of the United States. I'm not concerned about her being the first woman President. I simply believe that she will make a great President period. I like the fact that under pressure, she doesn't quiver and sticks to what she believes and what she knows.

I can recall the interrogation of her after the assassination of Americans in the 2012 Benghazi attack that took place on the evening of September 11, 2012. Islamic militants attacked the American diplomatic compound in Benghazi, Libya, killing U.S. Ambassador J. Christopher Stevens and U.S. Foreign Service Information Management Officer Sean Smith.

Ambassador Stevens was the first U.S. Ambassador killed in the line of duty since 1979. The attack has also been referred to as the Battle of Benghazi.

First of all, there was an intimation that she should have known or at least had done more to avoid this terrible tragedy and I believe that she did everything she could and had she known or had any indication that this cowardly act was about to occur, I'm certain that she would have done everything humanly possible to protect our people.

I'm also sure that Hillary was devastated by this horrible news and I could tell that she was greatly affected by it. But she handled herself well considering the circumstances and answered all the questions asked of her during the inquest. However, many were not satisfied with her response. She continued to answer to the best of her ability and she was unflappable and steadfast in her responses and all I can say is that I was then and continue to be very proud of her on so many different levels.

Needless to say, she has my vote. I don't see any other candidate out there that really gives her any competition.

As I look at the line up in both parties, I have to say…I would have to see some other folks throw their hats into the ring because the current group doesn't have the experience or the backbone from my standpoint to do the job that I believe Hillary will do for the country.

I'm not basing my beliefs on her husband's record nor the fact that she is a prior First Lady. I'm basing my opinion on what I've observed from a personal standpoint.

I believe her political record stands on it on and she was a great Senator and Secretary of State. Though I've read that she and President Obama don't really like one another, this is unimportant to me. It's not important for you to like someone.

You simply need to do your job despite whether you like them or not. However; I do believe that a lot of that was just talk and beliefs of people who wanted to see a rift between Hillary Clinton and President Obama.

Listed below are the candidates from the Republican Party vying for the Office of President in 2016.

REPUBLICAN PARTY CANDIDATES

- Skip Andrews ◄ **DECLARED**

- Michael Bickelmeyer ◄ **DECLARED**

- Kerry Bowers ◄ **DECLARED**

- Jeb Bush ◄ **DECLARED**

- Dr. Ben Carson ◄ **DECLARED**

- Dale Christensen ◄ **DECLARED**

- Chris Christie ◄ **EXPLORING**

- Ted Cruz ◄ **DECLARED**

- John Dummett, Jr. ◄ **DECLARED**

- Mark Everson ◄ **DECLARED**

- Carly Fiorina ◄ **DECLARED**

- Lindsey Graham ◄ **DECLARED**

- Chris Hill ◄ **DECLARED**

- Mike Huckabee ◄ **DECLARED**

- Michael Kinlaw ◄ **DECLARED**

- George Pataki ◄ **DECLARED**

- Rand Paul ◄ **DECLARED**

REPUBLICAN PARTY CANDIDATES

- Rick Perry   ◀ **DECLARED**

- Michael Petyo   ◀ **DECLARED**

- Marco Rubio   ◀ **DECLARED**

- Brian Russell   ◀ **DECLARED**

- Rick Santorum   ◀ **DECLARED**

- Donald Trump   ◀ **DECLARED**

While I certainly believed that the Republicans who have declared their candidacy for the Office of President clearly feel they are qualified for the Office, for the purpose of this book, I'll only elaborate on a few of them and those I believe could have a viable chance of being elected.

Carly Fiorina has an impressive resume, but she hasn't held any political office. She certainly has served in an advisory role to those in the Republican Party, yet, it is a big difference between advising versus having actually held a political office.

I liken it to consultants who are advising managers and supervisors. They can give all the advice they desire based upon their knowledge, but you have to actually walk in those positions to really understand what you need to be successful. And this is coming from someone who has been in both roles as a consultant and manager. Some people are talking about Rubio as a good fit for the Office of President and I would say not so fast.

Despite all the talk about Jeb Bush not being able to answer questions regarding whether or not he would have gone into Iraq had he known that there were no weapons of mass destruction, I would say that this isn't a reason to disqualify him. I believe that Jeb Bush has to reconcile with his brother the fact that a mistake was made by Bush 43rd.

We can't undo what happened, but Jeb needs to acknowledge it; be honest with his brother and get on with the business of running for President. I honestly believe that he would also be good in that office, but I don't believe he has the qualifications held by Hillary.

Additionally, I am unimpressed with Marco Rubio and there is nothing about him that rings out Presidential material to me. Some are comparing his experience to Barack Obama prior to him becoming President and I would say that the only comparison is that they both have been Junior Senators and hold law degrees.

However, Joe Biden would be great for the Office of President, but I believe he would be better as the Vice President to Hillary Clinton. In fact, I believe that theirs would be a dynamite pairing. Notice that I am not naming any other candidates because these are the only ones that stand out for me.

The current candidates for the 2016 Elections and Office of President in the Democratic Party are listed below. However, I have already indicated that Hillary Clinton is the most qualified and she has my vote.

DEMOCRATIC CANDIDATES

- Morrison Bonpasse   ◄ **DECLARED**

- Andy Caffrey   ◄ **DECLARED**

- Willie Carter   ◄ **DECLARED**

- Lincoln Chafee   ◄ **DECLARED**

- Hillary Clinton   ◄ **DECLARED**

- Martin O'Malley   ◄ **DECLARED**

- Bernie Sanders   ◄ **DECLARED**

- Doug Shreffler   ◄ **DECLARED**

- Michael Steinberg   ◄ **DECLARED**

- Robby Wells   ◄ **DECLARED**

There have been numerous claims that Barack Obama didn't have enough experience prior going into the White House.

Therefore, the next few pages outline his experience as a Senator when compared to other most likely candidates for President in 2016.

I have chosen Marco Rubio, Jeb Bush and of course, Hillary Clinton as the most viable candidates. After you review, their accomplishments, you be the judge as to whether or not you believe that Barack Obama had the necessary experience for the job. I have already given you my opinions of his expertise throughout this book.

SENATOR BARACK OBAMA ACCOMPLISHMENTS GOING INTO THE OFFICE OF PRESIDENT

- Senator Obama added three amendments to the Secure American and Orderly Immigration Act.

- The Lugar-Obama Cooperative Threat Reduction was introduced by Sen. Barack Obama, Sen. Dick Lugar and Sen. Tom Coburn and enacted in 2007. This bill expanded upon the successful Nunn-Lugar threat reduction, which helped secure weapons of mass destruction and related infrastructure in former Soviet Union states.

- Federal Funding Accountability and Transparency Act of 2006 was introduced into Congress by Senators Barack Obama and Coburn. It required the full disclosure of all entities or organizations receiving federal funds in 2007. The act passed into law and was signed by President Bush. The act had 43 co-sponsors, including John McCain.

- The Democratic Republic of the Congo Relief, Security, and Democracy Promotion Act specified US policy toward the Congo, and states that the US should work with other donor nations to increase international contributions to the African nation.

- This was the first federal legislation to be enacted with Barack Obama as its primary sponsor. After passage, Barack Obama toured Africa and traveled to South Africa, Kenya, Djibouti, Ethiopia and Chad. He also spoke forcefully against ethnic rivalries and political corruption in Kenya.

- In the first month of the 110th Congress, Barack Obama worked with Sen. Russ Feingold to pass the Honest Leadership and Open Government Act which amends and strengthens the Lobbying Disclosure Act of 1995.

- The changes made by Barack Obama and Feingold requires public disclosure of lobbying activity and funding, places more restrictions on gifts for members of Congress and their staff, and provides for mandatory disclosure of earmarks in expenditure bills. The House passed the bill, 411-8, on July 31. The Senate approved it, 83-14, on Aug. 2. At the time, Barack Obama called it "the most sweeping ethics reform since Watergate."

- Following the Republican-sponsored voter intimidation tactics seen in mostly African counties in Maryland during the 2006 midterm elections, Barack Obama worked with Sen. Chuck Schumer to introduce the Deceptive Practices and Voter Intimidation Prevention Act. This bill has been referred to the United States Senate Committee on the Judiciary. Barack Obama said of the bill, "This legislation would ensure that for the first time, these incidents are fully investigated and that those found guilty are punished."

- The Obama-McCain Climate Change Reduction Bill, which is co-sponsored by Sen. Joe Lieberman, I-Conn., would cut emissions by two-thirds by 2050.

- The Iraq War De-escalation Act of 2007 was introduced by Barack Obama. This binding act would stop the planned troop increase of 21,500 in Iraq, and would also begin a phased redeployment of troops from Iraq with the goal of removing all combat forces by March 31, 2008.

- Explaining the bill, Barack Obama said it reflects his view that the problems in Iraq do not have a military solution. "Our troops have performed brilliantly in Iraq, but no amount of American soldiers can solve the political differences at the heart of somebody else's civil war," Obama said.

- Barack Obama worked with Senator Kit Bond to limit, through the Amendments to the 2008 Defense Authorization Bill, the Pentagon's use of personality disorder discharges in the FY 2008 Defense Authorization bill.

- This provision would add additional safeguards to discharge procedures and require a thorough review by the Government Accountability Office. This followed news reports that the Pentagon inappropriately used these procedures to discharge service members with service-connected psychological injuries.

- "With thousands of American service members suffering day in and day out from the less visible wounds of war, reports that the Pentagon has improperly diagnosed and discharged service members with personality disorders are deeply disturbing," said Senator Obama. "This provision will add additional safeguards to the Department of Defense's use of this discharge and mandate a comprehensive review of these policies."

- Working with Sen. Hagel and Rep. Adam Schiff, Obama authored the Comprehensive Nuclear Threat Reduction provision, which would require the president to develop a comprehensive plan for ensuring that all nuclear weapons and weapons-usable material at vulnerable sites around the world are secure by 2012 from the threats that terrorists have shown they can pose.

- As an amendment to the State-Foreign Operations appropriations bill, a provision from the Obama-Hagel bill was passed by Congress in December 2007.

- Barack Obama said that it was imperative for the country to build and sustain a truly global effort under an aggressive timeline to secure, consolidate, and reduce stockpiles of nuclear weapons and weapons-usable material to keep them out of the wrong hands. He also believed that the comprehensive nuclear threat reduction plan required by this provision is an important step in that effort.

SENATOR MARCO RUBIO

ACCOMPLISHMENTS

- Marco Rubio voted against the Budget Control Act of 2011, which included mandatory budget cuts from "sequestration.

- In October 2011, Rubio co-sponsored a bill to reduce the size of Federal Government through attrition. This bill was not voted on in the senate.

- In November 2011, Rubio and Senator Chris Coons co-sponsored the American Growth, Recovery, Empowerment and Entrepreneurship Act (AGREE Act). The purpose of this act was to extend many tax credits and exemptions for businesses investing in research and development, equipment, and other capital as well as provide a tax credit for veterans who start a business franchise, allow an increase in immigration for certain types of work visas, and strengthen copyright protections.

- In 2012, Rubio introduced a bill, co-sponsored by Joe Manchin, to allow employers to be exempted from newly mandated coverage for contraception based on religious or moral grounds, but it wasn't adopted in the Senate.

- Rubio voted against the 2012 Fiscal Cliff Resolutions and received criticism for his position.

- In 2013, Rubio was part of the bipartisan "Gang of Eight" Senators that crafted comprehensive immigration reform legislation.

- In January 2013, Senator Rubio proposed a plan that would provide a path to citizenship for undocumented immigrants currently living in the United States.

- Rubio was chosen to deliver the Republican response to President Obama's 2013 State of the Union Address. It marked the first time the response was delivered in English and Spanish.

- On April 17, 2013, Rubio voted against an expansion of background checks for gun purchases.

- In May 2013, Rubio proposed the Regulation Costs to Small Businesses Act which would have required the Small Business Administration to conduct an annual study to estimate the total cost of regulations on small businesses.

- In July 2013, Rubio and Senator Ben Cardin introduced the Foreign Aid Transparency and Accountability Act. This bill would require federal agencies to monitor and regularly report on the performance of foreign assistance programs based on specified goals and metrics.

- In 2014, Rubio co-sponsored with Senator Mark Warner legislation to revise the process for calculating and collecting student loans.

- In 2014 Rubio asked Pope Francis "to take up the cause of freedom and democracy" in Cuba after helping negotiate the release of Alan Gross.

- In 2015 at a summit organized by Concerned Veterans for America Rubio said that the United States Department of Veterans Affairs was "simply buckling under the weight of its own bureaucracy" as he endorsed their proposal to open veterans care to private providers.

- Rubio has also taught a political science course at Florida International University during his U.S. Senate career.

JEB BUSH ACCOMPLISHMENTS

- Jeb Bush's most significant accomplishments are in the area of education. He made education reform a defining theme and introduced the "A+ Plan" to achieve consistent standardized testing across all schools.

- He eliminated social promotion programs and implemented a system of funding public schools based on a comparative grading system.

- Bush also championed school vouchers and charter schools in districts where public schools failed students but these initiatives failed to be implemented prior to him leaving office and continue to remain undone.

- However, Bush approved three new medical schools during his terms as Governor.

- Jeb Bush was more accessible to the people than prior Governors and remained popular throughout his terms with his Florida constituency.

- He was the first Republican governor to ever be re-elected to a second term in Florida history despite controversies during his governorship.

- Throughout his terms, Bush promoted a theme of non–discrimination and rewarding merit. He also appointed more highly qualified women, Africans and other minorities in top-level government positions than any prior Florida Governor.

HILLARY CLINTON

ACCOMPLISHMENTS

- Because of Republican obstruction, Hillary Clinton's healthcare plan, failed but it laid the ground work for today's Affordable Healthcare Act.

- Hillary had a primary role in the development of State Children's Health Insurance Program, which provides the much-needed state support for children whose parents can't afford nor provide them with adequate healthcare coverage.

- Hillary was instrumental in the creation of the Adoption and Safe Families Act and the Foster Care Independence Act.

- She successfully fought to increase research funding for prostate cancer and asthma at the National Institute of Health (NIH).

- Hillary spearheaded investigations into mental illness plaguing veterans of the Gulf War which is now referred to as the Gulf War Syndrome.

- She helped create the office on Violence Against Women at the Administrative Department of Justice.

- Hillary secured over $21 billion in funding for the World Trade Center redevelopment.

- Hillary commanded a lead role in the investigation of health consequences of first responders and drafted the first bill to compensate and offer the health services our first responders deserve (Clinton's successor in the Senate, Kirsten Gillibrand, passed the bill).

- She was instrumental in working out a bi-partisan compromise to address civil liberty abuses for the renewal of the U.S. Patriot Act.

- Hillary proposed a revival of the New Deal-era Home Owners' Loan Corporation to help homeowners refinance their mortgages in the wake of the 2008 financial disaster.

- She was a major proponent of sensible diplomacy which brought about a ceasefire between Hamas and Israel, and brokered human rights with Burma.

- Hillary oversaw free trade agreements with our allies such as Panama, Colombia, and South Korea.

- She was the most traveled Secretary of State to date.

- The Clinton Foundation, founded by Hillary and her husband, has improved the living conditions for nearly 400 million people in over 180 countries through its Initiative program.

This is only a few of Hillary Clinton's accomplishments. Her activism on behalf of women and children across the world is renowned. Her activism for raising the minimum wage and combating climate change is stellar.

CHAPTER ELEVEN

Impact of Racial Issues on Politics

Sadly, as I finish this book, another tragedy has occurred and this time it is the murder of nine African Americans by a young White man.

It is a very sad commentary when worshipers can't find peace in their sanctuary because of misguided ignorance and racist human beings. I said earlier that I believe that racism is at the root of many of the problems we have in the world today.

Unfortunately, my beliefs have once again been proven by this cowardly act. In this case, the man was welcomed in by the parishioners and worshipers who didn't have a clue about what was about to happen to them. They simply ushered this young man in and no doubt welcomed him with open arms.

The idea that someone can sit and worship with you and then stand with a loaded gun and shoot without any regard for human life simply because of the color of your skin is the most horrible and calculating thing that I can imagine. I am sick of the color and race issues and let me be clear, it's not only African Americans and Whites, racism runs rampant with all races and we have a problem in our own African American community as well.

There have been numerous occasions when I've had an African American make it a point to tell me about their light skin as though it afforded them some type of superiority over their darker skinned brothers and sisters. Get over yourself…I want to hear about how decent you are as a human being and what you have done to make the world a better place.

I could care less about the color of your skin. Get a clue people and stop tiptoeing around the issue of color and race. Let's have real dialogue and cut the bull!

If we don't we're going to see more Charleston's and other sick racial maladies in this beautiful world that we live in. It's not the world, guns or even technology that threatens our lives. It is the corrupt minds of those who have been raised to think that they're somehow better than other races.

And please don't be stupid enough to think that this is a South issue because it is not…I have had a lot of racial issues occur right here in California.

In fact, my worst experiences have occurred on the job where I was bypassed for promotions because I didn't quite fit the criteria that my bosses felt I should fit.

Yet, behind closed doors, White men and men of other races and high profile positions desired me and made passes at me.

If this book doesn't leave you with anything else, I hope it leaves you with the desire to get to the polls and vote for the person who is more likely than not to get this racial issue addressed with honest and open dialogue.

We can't just talk about this issue one more time and simply put it to rest. There has to be ongoing conversations about this issue or we'll be forever trapped in a world of ignorance, violence and turmoil.

ABOUT THE AUTHOR

Beverly Montgomery is a "go getter." She doesn't believe in sitting on your butt and complaining about things that are out of your control. She believes in trying different things and creating your own opportunities. Beverly says, sometimes, you have to toot your own horn and if necessary, get others to toot your horn as well. She says, "The worst thing you can do is to allow someone to make you feel inferior or inadequate."

Beverly makes it a point to step outside of her comfort zone and do things that she wouldn't have otherwise done. Along these lines, Beverly has authored over twelve books including historical, management, self-help, fiction, poetry, children and romance books.

She is self-taught in app development; possesses a MBA in Business Administration, BA in Management and Law; has received training and certification in Asbestos Management and she has over 35 years management and consulting experience.

Throughout her career, Beverly has continued to challenge herself including assuming responsibility for two separate and distinct business units. One unit was responsible for the sales, lease and acquisition of corporate real estate including the divestiture of power plants and the other involved engineering records management, contract management, mail service management, central telephone services, warehouse operations, reprographics, conference and sales management and administrative support. Though she doesn't advocate this for everyone, Beverly indicates that this was an exhilarating challenge and she enjoyed the challenge immensely.

Beverly also enjoys travelling and has made several trips to Europe and South America. Though she has enjoyed seeing and interacting with people in other parts of the world, her immediate focus is seeing more of the United States. She has already made three car trips throughout the South and plans to take more of these types of trips in the future.

Beverly Montgomery Books

On The Shoulders of Greatness – An historical account and tribute to those who have paved the way for all Americans.

Exploration, Empowerment and Advancement Booklet – This is an easy to read book about self -discovery and awareness. This book will enable readers to tap into their inner strengths and achieve successes that they never thought possible. Therefore, this book will change your life.

Exploration, Empowerment and Advancement Work Booklet - This workbook should be used in conjunction with the book "Exploration, Empowerment and Advancement because the workbook includes a variety of exercises that have been designed to assist you with achieving your desired goals

Imperfect People Managing in an Imperfect World - This book describes the lessons I have learned over the years due to imperfect people that I have encountered in the course of my personal and business life. The book provides tips on ways to overcome the obstacles that often occur with bad bosses who desire to do a good job but allow their personal baggage and problems to get in the way of themselves and others around them.

Pekepsy - This is a fictional book about a family, friends and associates who get caught up in a web of lies. It proves that hiding the truth from those you love can backfire on you and illustrates that wealth is good but money cannot buy you happiness.

A Burning Secret No More - An unexpected romantic interlude has a significant role in Sasha Broadway's desire to live her life without limits. She enjoys being in the company of men and she makes no excuses for it. But Sasha is holding a well-kept secret. Go with her on her journey of romance and love in A Burning Secret. But make sure you have the time because once you start reading this book you will not want to put it down!

Maxter The Magic Lion - Maxter the Magic Lion can do things that other lions in the jungle can't do so he is believed to have magical powers. One lion tries to find out why Maxter can do so many things. In the process, Maxter and all the other animals get a valuable lesson.

In The Light of Day - A fictional tale of one woman's mission to uncover secrets that have been kept by members of her family. Her attempt to discover the truth about herself results in a tale of deceit, infidelity and molestation. In the end, the story proves that what you do in the dark will surely come to light.

Back In the Game – A political book that provides my observations and assessment of our two major political parties and President Obama.

Authored under Pen Name: Honey Chocolate-Brown

- Mommy, Where Is Heaven?
- Mommy, Why Don't I Look Good in the Mirror?
- Mama Never Told Me
  In Deep Thought

BIBLIOGRAPHY

Origin of the Republican Party, US History.org, http://www.ushistory.org/goP/origins.htm (hosted by Independence Hall Associations in Philadelphia)

The first colored senator and representatives - in the 41st and 42nd Congress of the United States digital file from original print, Library of Congress
https://www.loc.gov/resource/ppmsca.17564/

Cornell West, Wikipedia, the Free Encyclopedia
https://en.wikipedia.org/wiki/Cornel_West

Tavis Smiley, Wikipedia, the Free Encyclopedia
https://en.wikipedia.org/wiki/Tavis_Smiley

Barack Obama Legislation Actions 2008, Outside the Beltway,
http://www.outsidethebeltway.com/obamas_legislative_accomplishments/

Hillary Clinton Accomplishments,Kstreet607.com, http://kstreet607.com/2015/04/13/heres-a-list-of-hillary-clintons-accomplishments-so-quit-saying-she-doesnt-have-any/

Jeb Bush Accomplishments, My Florida Representative.com
http://www.myfloridarepresentatives.com/jebbush.htm

Carla Fiorina, Wikipedia.org
https://en.wikipedia.org/wiki/Carly_Fiorina

Marco Rubio Accomplishments, Opportunity Lives.com
http://opportunitylives.com/marco-rubios-top-5-accomplishments-2/

The Watergate Scandal, History.com
http://www.history.com/topics/watergate

The Early Years of the Republican Party,
http://www.ushistory.org/gop/origins.htm

Dwight Eisenhower,
http://www.history.com/topics/us-presidents/dwight-d-eisenhower